# Poetry Journey through Pandemic

By Colin Self, June 2021

Pictures obtained from online ClipArt

Poetry written during forced lockdown due to the Coronavirus pandemic of 2020/21, collated for grandchildren, Amelia, Matthew, Isabella and possible others, to read in future years

# Poems

## The Covid-19 Effect

It's difficult to have an optimistic outlook with all this doom
Coronavirus has caused a tidal wave of pervading gloom
The invasive Covid-19's spawned the term self-isolation
Social distancing not being observed, causing consternation
Clubs, bars, gyms, schools, restaurants, shops all closed
Logistical problems to social structure of Britain now posed
The human spirit exhibits fortitude at times of such adversity
Seen many examples of moral, physical support and charity
Must not take risk unduly be sensible, resolve to be resilient
Remain positive and assuredly life once again will be brilliant

**STAY HOME. SAVE LIVES.**

**Help stop coronavirus**

1. **STAY** home as much as you can
2. **KEEP** a safe distance
3. **WASH** hands often
4. **COVER** your cough
5. **SICK?** Call ahead

General public health information

## Coronavirus Self-Isolation

Should we the promised directive of government trust
As they propose the over seventy's self-isolate must
This does not reflect the renowned British stiff upper lip
Keeping elderly indoors as coronavirus now takes grip
Will this generation the 24/7 curfew each day survive
Who will be responsible to check to see if dead or alive
Family members, neighbours, if any, expected to assist
Find people averting boredom by getting "Brahms & Liszt"
Avoiding visits to/from grandchildren or attending clubs
No senior citizens lunches as also banned from pubs
U3A, seniors cinema, Age UK will all soon be on hold
Unlike the younger generation they'll do as they're told
So how will the elderly cope with this enforced isolation
Not spend hours glued to You Tube, Xbox or PlayStation
Enjoy cerebral activities such as writing poetry or reading
And much better programmes on TV they'll be needing
Could Sky, Netflix, Amazon Prime, BBC be provided free
So enforced self-isolation a pleasure and less of a misery

## Staying Alive

Everybody get with it and start Jive talking
Listen to the Bee Gees don't go off walking
Stay home self-isolating and avoid Covid-19
Obey hand washing, social distancing routine
Everyone will have more chance of staying alive
As possible tragedy awaits those off for a drive
Extremely chilling when hear of so many dying
All over the world every nation is sadly crying

## Easter Isolation

Children excitably looking for the Easter bunny everywhere
No visit or hugs from Grandparents this weekend, it isn't fair
Coronavirus is causing mayhem there is no family meeting
Grandparents missing out, would love to visit if only fleeting
Picturing children enjoying milk chocolate eggs, so yummy
Hoping brothers, sisters share eggs with daddy and mummy
Don't save Grandparents any as can't see end of self-isolation
Wait to enjoy chocolates together on next family occasion

## A New Beginning

Walking through woodlands can see and feel spring in the air
Leaves on the trees, birds singing, flowers blooming everywhere
Notice only few people go by and these days none hand in hand
Need for social distancing everybody now begins to understand
The population hoping that soon there'll be end to this lockdown
And can again find their smiles and optimism, remove sad frown
But can't see end of self-isolation and definitely won't be soon
Afterwards likely new way of living to which will have to attune

## A Bevy of Beauty

Below the window appears an exquisite apparition very serene
There in the bright sunlight enhancing the familiar river scene
Not the bright yellow daffodils nor tulips dancing in the breeze
No, a much more delightful vision for this lonely soul to tease
Two attractive ladies soaking up the sunshine chatting together
Keeping the requisite distance apart in the warm sunny weather
Covid-19 and the need for self-isolation restricts all daily routine
Peered casually out of the window not sure whether to intervene
Equably remarked that a bevy of beauties beneath my balcony
An alliteration, fully appreciated by the ladies gazing up at me
Suggested a poem be written about belles lounging on the lawn
Not unsurprisingly greeted with disbelief, laughter, a stifled yawn
So here are a few words in a poem composed just for those two
Thankyou both for sitting under the window augmenting the view

## No Tennis Today

Did not believe I would feel so bad
Or get to be this morose and sad
How could I end up being this low
What is the root of this tale of woe
More glitches with friend's female
A futile romance of which to regale
Nothing so simple and ingenuous
The causes are even more tenuous
Couldn't book on to tennis session
DL app part cause of depression
Coronavirus creating complications
Four player limit, basis of frustrations
Must try to book earlier in the week
If pleasure of tennis on Friday seek

## Experiencing Self - Isolation

Look through the window, sun shining but nobody there
Remembering that old adage to take time, stop and stare
Now seems self-isolation has life as we know it, halted
No football, cricket not starting, wives, girlfriends exulted
Debating who should do the food shopping every day
No toilet rolls, sanitiser, bread but lots of booze, hooray
Find Lego, cards, boardgames and jigsaw without delay
Living alone, maybe crosswords, solitaire or patience play
Perhaps write poetry, certain most couldn't do any worse
Collate covert thoughts, ideas, memories and pen a verse
Astonish family, friends, lovers with those intimate notions
Expounding such feelings may alleviate pent up emotions
Many families will have little income and dread tomorrow
Before this pandemic ends there'll be much more sorrow
Health of you, family, friends, everybody across the nation
Is more important than this complaining about self-isolation
Look forward to happier days when coronavirus is no more
Stay safe, remain positive, until Covid-19 becomes folklore

## Geriatric Tennis

Another Friday and no social tennis unfortunately
Not been able to enjoy any tennis at all just lately
Incompatible with the Covid-19 social distancing
Is there an alternative which maybe as enticing?
Manual work in garden or slap dash decorating
To some may possibly seem just as invigorating
Though for those without garden or live in a flat
There is less opportunity to work out doing that
Going for a stroll around town or parks nearby
Less satisfying than tennis one's time to occupy
Need opportunity to enjoy tennis with adept play
Hitting consistent winners to everybody's dismay
Playing skilful strokes, mostly consistent returns
Consistency, exactly what a social player yearns
Coach encouraging and not mocking any mistake
When play again these over 70s legs will ache
Coach enthusiastically exhorting players to move
Praising effort when his derision they disapprove
Some not politely informing him what he can do
Others hobbling round court, shots often miscue
See them miss yet another easy overhead smash
All look the part and at their age still cut a dash
Looking forward to when Friday sessions resume
Not until social distancing is relaxed, we presume

## It's Only Logical

Wishing this Coronavirus would go away
So everybody can happily go out to play
Social distancing and wearing of masks
Makes it challenging doing routine tasks
Holidays no fun if, on return, quarantine
When will they find an effective vaccine
The economy is already spiralling down
When will we see again a bustling town
Children at last going back into schools
Teacher unions say a decision by fools
Denying youngsters schooling is unjust
As everybody agrees education a must
Subsidised dining has been enjoyed
Restaurants and bars, coffers buoyed
Now need all employees to go to work
Essential staff did not their roles shirk
NHS frontline staff managed situation
For which they have a grateful nation
Let's hope beaches are soon deserted
And no more the law will be perverted
By individuals going to a crowded rave
Which may lead others to early grave
Why aren't people aware, responsible
As Spock would say "it's only logical"!

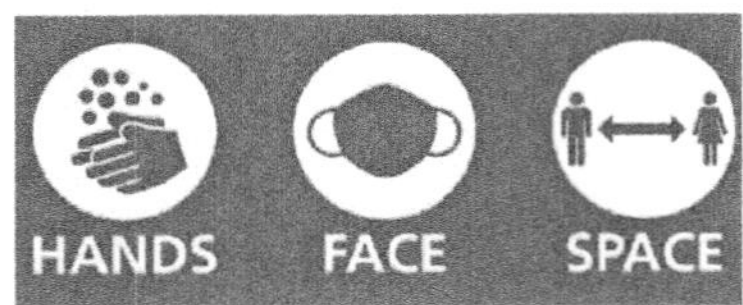

## Abnormality

Suffer from a very rare disease
Do not feel sorry for me please
Although most annoying malady
I do not seek any sort of remedy
Perceived as a strange deformity
Some say a peculiar irregularity
Because of this unique anomaly
Become somewhat of an oddity
Hope you'll forgive this deviation
It is from an earlier malformation
Though some say an eccentricity
I would define as an idiosyncrasy
So to regain some sense of reality
Could just call this an abnormality
Covid-19 changed this conclusion
Added an even greater confusion
Coronavirus proved to be endemic
Maybe malaise result of pandemic
Disrupting the olfactory functions
Offered by many various unctions
Covid-19 affects all with impunity
Few show signs of herd immunity

## Coping with Lockdown

Converse with me please just talk about your life
Prefer to hear of exciting good times, not of strife
Everybody's experiences include ups and downs
Times cherished, others contrary, full of frowns
With this Covid-19 need conversation full of fun
Forget those days of dejection, fears oh so glum
Social media providing anecdotes and cartoons
Play music, try to remember lyrics of fave tunes
Seek new activities, as unlikely any work today
Nor able to watch cricket or football teams play
No eating out, coffee mornings, drinks in nice bar
Gyms, tennis clubs, golf courses shut, it's bizarre
Walks outside especially in groups been banned
Visits to the cinema or theatre cannot be planned
Self-isolation, social distancing, new paradigms
Difficult going shopping in these uncertain times
When will lockdown, paralysis of society cease
Only if Coronavirus deaths markedly decrease

## Lockdown Ineffective

Covid-19 lockdown drove us all nearly insane
Especially when weather predominantly rain
Did not seem so bad when sun shone brightly
Restrictions could be borne much more lightly
Why did so many the social distancing ignore
Enjoying days on beach amidst public uproar
Not waiting for derestriction to be put in place
Forgetting applauding for the NHS, a disgrace
As lockdown by government is gradually eased
Restaurants, shops, pubs, gyms, very pleased
Also now all vulnerable permitted to socialise
As elderly fear of loneliness or worse exorcise
Not sure life will ever return to normality again
Many jobs lost and borrowed monies to regain
The coronavirus pandemic abated not gone
Now struggle to save our economy has begun

## Mankind will Prevail

It was the same in 1665 as told in Pepys diary of that day
The public ignored edicts and went out for revelry and play
Despite the plague raging through the whole of our society
Many people refused to behave with sense and propriety
History repeating itself, total disregard of social distancing
A public deaf to the pleas of scientists or just not listening
Allowing Coronavirus to spread uninhibited across the land
How many lives must be lost before the morons understand
Devastating families, putting unnecessary burden on NHS
Why a minority believe they are immune is anybody's guess
Now politicians are ranting why few ventilators, no PPE gear
Rather than make constructive comment and help stem fear
Our innovative engineers designing equipment that's desired
Factories changing production lines to make what's required
Of course government systems overwhelmed, cannot cope
And unfortunately many must feel there's really little hope
Against unprecedented challenge the human race won't fail
Yes, resourceful, indomitable spirit of mankind shall prevail

## Lockdown Woes

Everybody is trying to avoid this malign virus
Which is making society irrational, nervous
There is no simple remedy using an antibiotic
This coronavirus is proving to be very exotic
Also it's very contagious or possibly infectious
Whichever, the consequences are atrocious
The world now is at the centre of a pandemic
Unfortunately the virus has become endemic
Only protection offered is simply self-isolation
Which has led to much anger and frustration
Little testing only ineffectual track and trace
Hence draconian lockdown we have to face
Though this may help the health of the nation
Causes leisure industry and business vexation
Everybody struggling living with this unreality
Desperately wanting to enjoy again normality
Until scientific research identifies a vaccine
We will suffer more lockdown and quarantine
Illogical unfounded suppositions expounded
Politicians and public all utterly confounded
Misinterpreted data has led to consternation
All Government experts want is approbation
Nobody wants anymore Covid 19 mortalities
Nor suffering from gloomy economic realities
Restaurants, shops, pubs must be reopened
So life can begin again and become jocund
Government concerned Xmas will be missed
Nobody will be able to get Brahms and Liszt

## Christmas Lockdown or Not

Writing Christmas rhymes in November, seems strange
With Coronavirus all now have their lives to rearrange
No decorations nor Xmas tree brightening up the house
With lockdown no friends or family all quiet as a mouse
Of course, most children will already be on countdown
Society too but more likely for an end to this lockdown
Covid -19 has been the vexatious issue of present day
For younger generation just a nuisance precluding play
Government trying to lift lockdown in time for Christmas
Or will more "scientific data" preclude festivities for us?
Only "turkeys" are advocating for lockdown to continue
Not grasping restaurants/pubs/business losing revenue
Resulting in a lost generation of resentful unemployed
Our once thriving social and economic life destroyed
So will there be a Christmas in 2020 for us to enjoy
Or will Boris' delusional cohorts continue us to annoy

## Govts Christmas Message

It's Christmas time and we are all really afraid
Not of coronavirus but way our lives degrade
Subjected to tier system which ill thought out
Served with fines if dare guidelines to flout
Discord within Tory ranks is understandable
Asking why livelihoods thought dispensable
Printing monies to prop up an economy ailing
Policies which to the public are clearly failing
Daily number of deaths “with Covid” recorded
Not deaths “caused by Covid” deemed sordid
Every death is a tragedy to people somewhere
Causes suffering that we are all only too aware
But there is an old adage which says the cure
Is sometimes worse than the disease, I'm sure
But believe these wise words are now ignored
Though to many in hardship will touch a chord
So Christmas will for most be very quiet affair
As Government says family gatherings beware
Too many congregating to enjoy the festivities
May be arrested for allowing serious felonies
Yes, be accused of causing death of a relative
A greeting given which is anything but festive
So remember the guidelines, don't break rules
Ensure a Merry Christmas, avoid being fools

# The Coronavirus Effect

The path we tread regularly does twist and turn
Often can't reach the aspirations that we yearn
A lifetime opting for various pathways to follow
Making life choices for a future we do not know
Equably facing experiences both good and bad
Letting go of some that could make us feel sad
Finding moments of tangible happiness to enjoy
Trying to avoid unimportant things which annoy
Opt not to worry that bathroom is really a mess
Nor about those smelly dishes in sink obsess
Not disaster that windows have lost their shine
The children's unkempt bedrooms are just fine
Everybody is well aware how fast time does fly
And that even the best laid plans often go awry
A happy, contented life is for all what's desirous
Which has cruelly been affected by Coronavirus
Many hospitalised and sadly friends, family lost
For all, pandemic has come at rather high cost
Cheerful, optimistic, caring attitude is required
More sanguine poetry to inspire is now desired

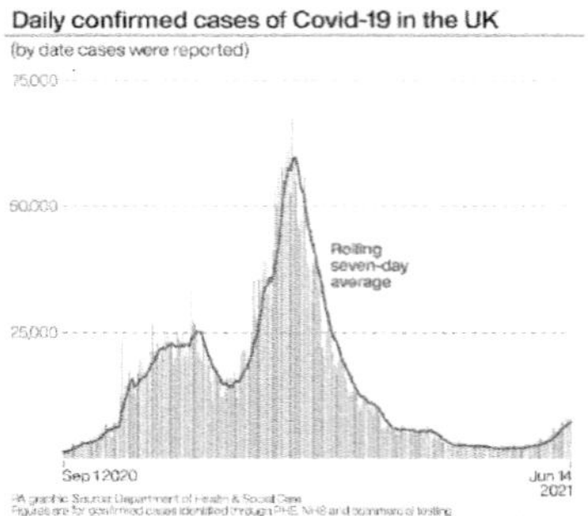

## Christmas on Pause

We might as well face it no Christmas this year
The government advisers have made a pigs ear
Lost grasp of good old fashioned common sense
Imposed draconian rules at country's expense
Promulgating false stats and data most suspect
Result is loss of societies sympathy and respect
No wonder by many, guidelines being subverted
PPE monies to government crony's diverted
MPs say likely have to put Christmas on pause
No happy visits by children to jolly Santa Claus
Families being kept apart, self-isolate they say
Children listening for jingle bells of Santa's sleigh
No exercise for the reindeer delivering presents
Covid pandemic disrupting our Christmas events
Buying online, no store visits with carol singing
No visit from Santa who's himself quarantining
Empty shops and stores, toys, presents unsold
Some won't miss the trek to mall if truth be told
Forget decorations, meeting friends or going out
No turkey, mince pies, pudding or brussel sprout
Twinkling Christmas lights will seem less bright
Until obtain vaccine with which this virus to fight
Maybe in the New Year of this virus we'll be free
And people's lives can return to some normality

## Covid Christmas Tale

Christmas time
Sleigh bells chime
Mistletoe
Kissing, no
No carol singing
Church bells ringing
Spirits, ale
Next day, pale
Covid pandemic
Scientific polemic
Eyes all red
Aching head
Biased stats
No caveats
Difficulty meeting
Spatial seating
Track, locate
Self-isolate
Benign process
Locale assess
Brass bands play
Hopefully, someday
Lives lost
Economic cost
Bearded Saint
Fat and quaint
Sisters, brothers
Fathers, mothers
Can't be with us
Avoiding virus
Seasons joys
Books and toys
Fun of giving
Joy of living
Crackers, rhymes
Few pantomimes
Season of sharing
Time for caring
From a distance
Govt insistence
Gifts unending
Excess spending
Up at dawn
Stifling yawn
Happy cries
Mince pies
Vaccine found
Safe and sound

*Remembering good friend, Bill Gray*

## Hide Innate Fears

New Years eve of 2020 and was very early to bed
No company, drinks, laughter, quite quiet instead
Covid-19 still rife at end of depressing, trying year
Leaving so many with sadness and so little cheer
Everybody hoping that 2021 will improve for us
As the vaccine is distributed to control the virus
Hoping by Easter will have much greater freedom
All need to survive few more months of boredom
Many will have difficulty coping with this situation
Lots of families and friends confronting destitution
Facing a partial lockdown with continued furlough
No chance for jobs or businesses to start to grow
Deaths attributed to Coronavirus continue to rise
But is desolation of economy an advisable exercise
Is there any proof hospitality heightens virus spread
Or are scientific assessments based purely on dread
Whatever the true facts are, everybody now in tiers
And public must for a little longer curb innate fears

## More Cheerful Poetry

A friend suggested writing poetry more cheerful
Asked why verses always tended to be mournful
But poems reflect the times that we are enduring
Understand more light hearted words reassuring
However, want to retain some realism in message
Not intention all trepidations and fears to assuage
Many of our older generation becoming scared
Accepting of stats or obfuscation aren't prepared
PHE fearing hospitals very soon will be over run
Second wave was forecast but Nightingales gone
Expensive Track and Trace not effectively in use
Hoping vaccination roll out will pandemic reduce
Trying to write upbeat for my elderly geriatric mate
Deliberately offering sentiments for all to cogitate
Into another lockdown, doesn't confer much cheer
Really only find solace in wine, gin, whisky or beer
Writing poetry can only succeed with drink to hand
Like culinary skills, literary ones lubrication demand

## Happier Rhymes

Would like to start dreaming of a much happier tomorrow
How is that possible when many now incur so much sorrow
Covid 19 is robbing all generations of viable contented life
Leaving families struggling to cope with unparalleled strife
Many facing much anguish as lose loved ones or livelihood
Difficult to dream of better days from where they are stood
Writing of realism should not one's literary integrity impugn
We are all in this together is for some a presumptuous tune
To break yoke of Coronavirus is Governments main mission
As economy on its knees and facing a double dip recession
Some battling loneliness despite ostensibly living comfortably
Too many individuals flouting lockdown, acting irresponsibly
Would love to write words and verses to cheer up our nation
Avoiding sentiments which from some bring condemnation
Everybody desperately looking for an end to Covid pandemic
Scientists providing vaccines which believe will be systemic
When rollout is quickly and effectively for everyone achieved
Then perhaps rhymes about happier future can be conceived

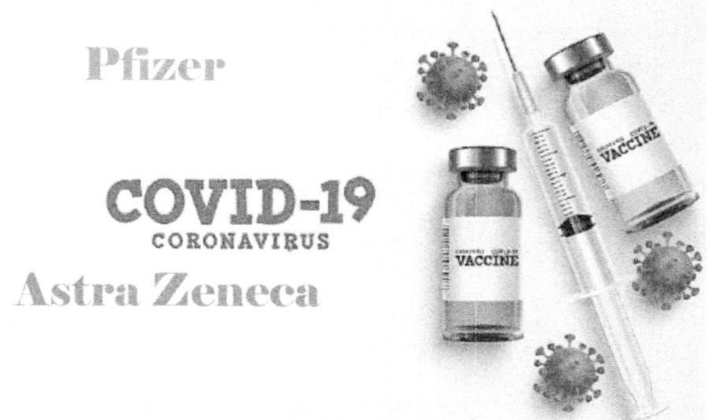

## Lockdown Diversion

Spanish was a language previously had to learn
Often found the spoken word difficult to discern
The written word favoured as easier to translate
Have time to consider, read again and deliberate
Now self-isolation gives opportunity to learn again
Back in the 1980's a degree of fluency did attain
Though had difficulty with noun before adjective
And verbs with no direct object called intransitive
The past, present, future verbs made little sense
Said "ayer o manaña" before using present tense
Invariably subject and predicate were misplaced
Usually occurred when trying to interpret in haste
Verb suffixes changing for pronouns you're using
Knowing correct gender for words also bemusing
Study late in the evening through Duolingo online
Helped by imbibing tot of whiskey or glass of wine
Words, phrases used in conversation memorised
Spelling especially diacritical marks emphasised
Need weeks of self-isolation to improve learning
Yet resolution of Covid-19 is what I am yearning
Will acquisition of language skill be tried in Spain
Could life ever be normal, package hols by plane
Once businesses, restaurants, bars, shops trading
And Covid-19 under control and far less pervading
How long before this doom and gloom will vanish
Until that time will continue daily dose of Spanish

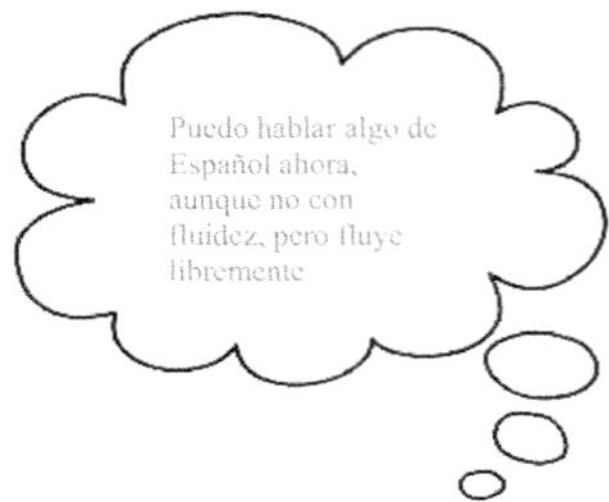

## Pandemic Pandemonium

This pandemic is dire and getting worse
Many praying will avoid ride in a hearse
Are these thoughts rather over dramatic
Not if working in NHS or senile geriatric
Self-isolation difficult when live all alone
Lucky ones family or friends them phone
Some link with outside world is needed
As long as social distance fully heeded
Timely for some on TV lots of football
Other programmes screened abysmal
May seem rather provocative comment
Loss of the old TV comedies do lament
Some wouldn't get past the PC brigade
Sexist, racist and worst of all man made
Netflix, Amazon, Disney, Sky new trend
Many think BBC licence an unfair spend
Unlikely that any big change is imminent
Must endure continued biased comment
Over handling of coronavirus pandemic
And Brexit which luckily now is academic
Unsupportive reporting on Govt policies
Giving time to other unreliable fallacies
Will BBC ever become apolitical again
With reporters of much higher acumen
Be optimistic about panacea on horizon
Which promises virus will soon be gone
Vaccination rollout going extremely well
Can thoughts of future not on past dwell
Also have escaped European shackles
Such comment will raise some hackles
Last year we saw only doom and gloom
As virus, capacity of NHS did consume
Already benefits of independence shown
Purchase decisions on vaccines we own
To control, eradicate epidemic we must
Before welfare, economy of UK is bust

## Not Viable Proposition

Who would really want to be young once again
With Covid 19, lockdowns, unemployment pain
Know aches, stiff limbs and being unable to run
Hamper seniors ability to get about and have fun
Not being allowed to go out freely to pub or gym
When you are young and energetic must be grim
Theatre, cinema, sports, partying all now denied
Social distancing most important as so many died
Cities, regions register increase in Covid cases
As a winter of despondency, discontent UK faces
Society soon will have Brexit with which to cope
No wonder many now are beginning to lose hope
Of course older generation will to two wars refer
Relating of sacrifices and hardships that did occur
But in recent years of enhanced communications
And ever increasing aspirations and expectations
So difficult for leaders to give rational explanation
Unable to manage pandemic without obfuscation
Quote science, deem statistical data are definitive
Bereft of common sense, solutions unimaginative
Public now reproach leaders for political posturing
Never offering much hope and antipathy fostering
Senior citizens and the young all probably agree
Lockdowns unviable must try to rescue economy

## New Year Tiers

January first was beginning of New Year
Everybody wishing for loads more cheer
Previous nine months was real nightmare
As the prevalent Covid-19 did us all scare
Suffering in tiers followed by a lockdown
Caused lots of people to display a frown
Total Covid deaths recorded, horrendous
Despite NHS effort that was tremendous
All hopes now resting on vaccine roll out
No more pandemic rules for some to flout
Normal life to resume for a number of us
But many will be suffering after this virus
Lost jobs and businesses not now viable
Significant cost of pandemic undeniable
Strength of purpose now must stimulate
And wartime spirit of forefathers emulate

## Lockdown Dread

Every lockdown felt like the living dead
Dire thoughts imagined filled with dread
Many months of coping with coronavirus
Which has impacted the lives of all of us
Pain and hurt for everybody still goes on
Nobody thought it would ever last so long
Now a lot less carefree laughter is heard
Social gatherings have all been deferred
Not sure when holidays can be arranged
Everybody's lives all drastically changed
Living through an extremely strange time
Writing simple words which almost rhyme
Recollecting emotions and how kept sane
When tough for any normal life to sustain
Crucial, virulent pandemic was contained
Thus populace by lockdowns constrained
Too many did never to guidelines adhere
Despite infections, deaths being so severe
With vaccination programmes in full swing
At last the "Fat Lady" can come out to sing

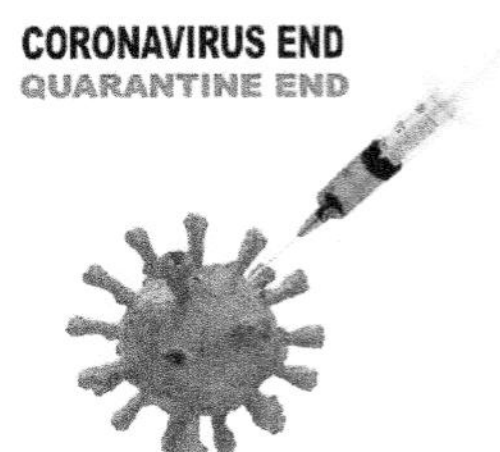

## Verses Forlorn

Recently my verses have been rather forlorn
From Coronavirus and lockdown been born
Now live with more optimism on the horizon
As some of the public able to get vaccination
Can write poetry of the uplifting happier kind
As life gets back to some normality we'll find
Be able to socialise greet with a hand shake
No more behind those face masks will quake
Call at the pub with friends for a beer or two
Attend live gigs, the theatre, cinema and zoo
Better weather will also demeanour enhance
All will of such opportunities take the chance
Permit travel around UK and also overseas
Freedom of movement will everyone please
Sit with picnic watching cricket on the green
Part of the British way of life an idyllic scene
Better days really can't come round too soon
And definitely enable us to hum happier tune
Many need to overcome sadness of lives lost
As govt strive to reconcile the economic cost

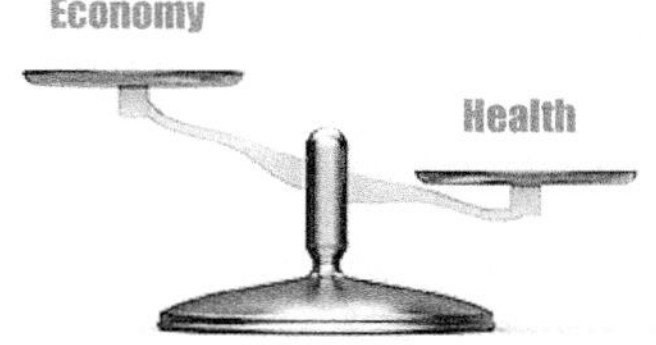

## An End to Lockdown

Want to write poems that convey more happiness
No tales of woe, disappointment not even distress
Life has been difficult with Covid-19 and lockdown
Most valid reason to be morose and wear a frown
Now possible to write cheerfully and optimistically
Relate tales of society behaving more altruistically
Aiding those struggling to manage with being alone
Remembering to listen be sympathetic not to moan
A smile and caring word calms any imagined fears
Accept at times can do little to prevent angry tears
Now need poems to foretell of future joyous times
The success of vaccine rollout one of the first signs
Lifting of frustrating lockdown now drawing nearer
With future though still uncertain becoming clearer
Soon able to socialise freely with family and friends
Tough government measures have paid dividends
Poems will tell of fun evenings in bars or out dining
Enjoying theatre and cinema trips our silver lining
Much happier verses telling of more whimsical era
Positive poetry could be part of my literary nirvana

## Restrictions Relaxed

I wake up with another day to face
Hope will be in much happier place
Make my own time for me to spend
Enjoy moment with a special friend
Genial dining and drinking together
Enjoy walks in the summer weather
Hoping soon to have few short trips
Be good after last year of hardships
Lockdown prevented any socialising
Not seeing loved ones demoralising
A future is now there for all to relish
With someone whom you do cherish
Untroubled days of fun and laughter
Life awaiting us after Covid disaster

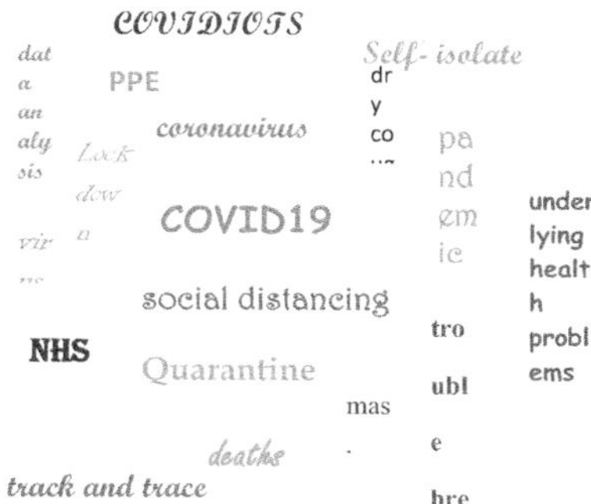

## Life after Covid-19

That Covid-19 pandemic did us a life deny
Now ponder on those days that passed by
Struggling to cope as stay home our routine
Recall hospitals full and death toll obscene
Now envisaging freedom after the lockdown
Happy avoided potential nervous breakdown
Too often suffered imposed social distancing
Many found required restrictions distressing
Particularly individuals who were living alone
Feeling their castle was a prison not a home
Having survived privation now feel liberated
Lifting of restrictions so much less debilitated
Dreams held in abeyance can now come true
Return to happier life that we all once knew
Replacing those fears of a future full of strife
With a very contented, fulfilling, satisfying life

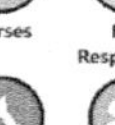

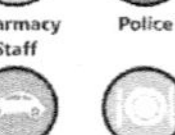
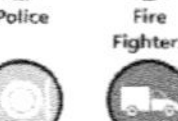

# Coronavirus Pandemic

*Twenty plus years or maybe even more*
*You will be recalling Covid days of yore*
*When pandemic was everybody's curse*
*And Grandpa wrote of that time in verse*

*Stay Safe*
*Social distancing, Wash your hands*
*Lockdown, Quarantine, Vaccination*

Printed in Great Britain
by Amazon